1.


The Friend


Just outside the circle of my life,

Someone is watching.

Reviewing all the good times and the strife

But only watching

Into that circle He cannot reach or touch

But only watch

Wanting to help me, to change things, so much!

Bye and bye the dawning of the light

Causes me to have some small insight

Then I reach out through the wall,

That really wasn't there at all,

And touch the person watching.

2.

## Soul-light

A lovely sunlit day too bright, to harbor

The cobwebs in the dungeon of my soul

The sun creeps through the cracks of decay

That was once my happiness.

For a while I bask in the warm brightness.

Dark thoughts cower in far corners,

Unable to surface through the fierce light


Soon the sun sets.

I keep its memory alive in my heart.

Dark soul eating memories are drowned

Too weak to leap into the consciousness of my mind

The silent hours creep by, those cowering destroyers

Try to ruin the night; I fight in silent combat,

Sometimes I win.

3.


## The Horse Rule


It's expensive to keep a horse,

It needs hay and shoes and brushing too

Only special feed will do.


If you rent the land for it to stay

You'd better have the means to pay.

While your brain is in an addle,

Remember you have to buy a saddle.


There's one rule to remember of course

Don't put the cart before the horse.

4.


<u>Of Leaves</u>


Winter is in the air...

The sweet smelling orange and gold leaves fall

Will soon lay down their lives;

That spring things may thrive again

From beneath their blackened shapes


Tarry not on that grim thought; of those warm colors

Beneath a blanket of sparkling virgin snow

One surprising day the warmth of spring returns

The newborn spears gently peek through the blanket

Provided by last years faded leaves

5.

## <u>Twin Babies</u>

They are so darling so alike

Two acorns from an Oak

I soak up the pleasure of their company

And receive soft kisses and hugs

From pail skinned arms and fragile fingers.

Chocolate tresses flow around vanilla faces

And sad blue eyes show concern

For your age and ask:

Are you going to die grandma?

I laugh and assure them not now

But someday a long, long, time from now I will,

Because everything eventually does

Two little faces close to mine

Whispering secrets, to tease the other

Cuddling, one on each knee

I succumb to my hearts rapture.

6.

<u>Sunday Guest</u>

A True Story

Grandma's buns smelled so good!

With added cheese made top rate food.

An egg alongside, a gorgeous sight

Really raised our appetite


On Grandma's window ledge we left

The crumbs we didn't eat.

All the birds, for miles around

Knew of Grandma's treat


We were sure the same ones came each day,

(And often heard my Grandma pray)

They liked to sit there in the sun.

Soon she loved them, everyone.


On Sunday morning, nine it was

I remember very clearly because

We'd put out the crumbs and were breaking our fast,

The birds were eating first to last

7.


Sunday Guest continued


Then much to our joy and delightful surprise,

A bird came to breakfast in front of our eyes.

He hopped 'round the table as calm as you please,

Pecking at tidbits of crumbs and of cheese


I tried not to fidget to hold up my breath.

I tried not to sneeze and so scare him to death.

Then he jumped on my plate and gave me the eye.

(So small and so precious, this tiny brave guy)


Then he wriggled his tail

And took three hops, not two,

Then out of the window

He happily flew.

8.


The Shade Tree


How long that tree has stood

Its branches; shading from the sun;

Ants and worms and Violets

A tired worker sits

To mop his brow and

With his hand upon that crinkled bark

Admires its strength and beauty


Lives and times change and pass,

The tree oblivious

Gentle, sometimes harsh, winds

Rustle leaves, bend the sturdy boughs

Strong, yet supple, taking from the earth

Giving of its self,

To those beneath its boughs

9.


## Wanderer


When the deep dark night is sparkling

With stars unseen by day

The wanderer gazing upward

Wonders why he went away.


He gazes at the million stars,

Profoundly does he ponder

Where he fits in the ladder of life,

And why his feet must wonder.

10.


<u>After the Coming</u>


The prairie grass goes on, endlessly.

Heat waves move in the air.

A small brown bird busily ignores me.

On this small rise

With rocks, one tree, and me

Where I can see what is there.

The white man has come.

I see nothing.

11.


<u>Metis</u>


Many times a hundred years have passed

Since our blood was of one race.

Still we banish the thought and pretend,

That we are the children of those first ones

Their blood is stronger than white,

Their spirit goes on forever,

And lives in me and those like me

We carry the spirit of the old ways.

Only our skin is white.

12.


## After Death


Aye, this night I have died.

I went not alone, for He was at my side.

As I left I saw your grief and tears.

I wish you could know I had no fears.

I wish you had spoken those dear words

My ears to hear as darkness fell,

That you loved me, as I had loved you well

Too late now, another journey to start

Good-bye. Goodbye my dearest heart.

13.


The Last Meeting Place

To a pet


When I approach the golden gates of heaven

It will be you mine eyes be searching for.

I know you will be waiting

In that long line of devoted creatures

Waiting for me,

Then we will spend eternity

Side by side

14.


<u>Life's End</u>


There he lies, in all those years

Of peaceful slumber

Enjoying? What we cannot have on earth.

Careless with his life!

He leaves our asunder.

His own dreams, he took from himself!

Where now, is his thoughtless mirth?

15.


<u>Love Letter</u>


Writing a letter to you

The sky here is very blue

The finches are singing

The seagulls are winging

While sharing these thoughts with you

My heart remains true

As I'm writing to you

I think I hear chapel bells ringing

My hearts all awhirl

When I think of my girl

And what the future is bringing.

<u>16.</u>


<u>Passing</u>


If you should hear of me the news "she's dead",

Think not of me in sorrow, only that I've fled.

From all the worst that living offered me,

And took only the sweetest memories of thee


As I hover in some special place, and touch you

Now and then, with the image of my earthly face,

Tis only that I do so from above, to remind you

That once this face did love

<u>17.</u>

## <u>I Wonder</u>

If despair follows you into the afterlife

Then hear my moans.

If agony of unsolved pain

Accompanies us into the spirit world

Then hear my groans.

When you wake up in the night

And think, what made you wake in fright;

Or, when the wind changes from sighing

And begin a rasping crying, think

Of souls who died with no resolve

Too late, your dire deeds to solve

A cold damp chill creeps on your skin,

And you alone mull on your sin.

18.


Farewell


Don't cry over me,

Don't weep my dear friend.

This new beginning is

Not just an end.

I'm simply leaving

All that misery and kind

To walk up those stairs

On feet I've left behind.

19.


<u>Our Lifetime Passing</u>


We must rush

Headlong

Into our tomorrows


The days that are ours

Are fast depleting

Quickly! Make new joys

From old sorrows

Experiences

Are only seconds fleeting

20.


<u>Prints</u>


Silver horses in the blowing snow

Leave no hoof prints as they go

A sound, in the winter, to listen I pause

And look to the rooftops

There is no Santa Clause!


My footprints are left in the sand by the sea,

Then they are gone, all that's left, is me.

We think that we see

We think that we know

Then we leave behind nothing

Like prints in the snow

21.


<u>Trail Rider</u>


I sat behind the thick mane

And watched the flow of movement there

I watched the ears that ever flickered

To side and forward, I followed his stare,

For my gallant mount watched everywhere.


The snow creaked loudly where he walked,

Down the mountain trail that wound along

Through stands of Fir, where winter's rills

Bubbled and voiced their watery song.


That sweet scent of warm and sweating coat,

Caught me up and warmed the air around.

I, sitting high above the snow,

Enjoyed the Mountain View and horsey sound

Soon the trail became a well-used track.

The ranch buildings appeared, no going back.

All that's left to do, is hang the saddle up for now,

Cool my horse and hang the tack.

The trails will be there another day,

And we'll be back.

22.


Killer


Can you not hear?

The silent cry of pain,

From that which you have shot?

And will ne'er breathe life again?

What kind of man are you, who stone faced calmly sits the corps

And wipes the blood red blade on virgin snow?


The lazy gaze of death stares up at you,

Recording your image in its last luster,

Still, you do not quake!

What kind of man are you?

Your woman awaits your coming, no hunger there.

Your teepee full of store bought goods,

Hoarded like bones in a lair


You do not hunt with pony, bow and skill.

You ride your metal monster, cruising for a kill.

Unaware, your high powered rifle leaves the dead.

23.


Killer continued


What kind of women takes you to her bed?

Go away killer, lose yourself

To a more modern whore

The earth and her creatures don't need you

Anymore!

## Friendship the Great Redeemer

I asked a friend to supper

She lives alone.

I turned the television down to a more sober tone

As I know that the noise it screeches

Annoy her train of thought.

And in its noisy constants, I've forgot.

We sit with our own voices

Eating what meal there is and

Not complaining but enjoying choices.

We are comfortable in our friendship

And expect nothing else from each other

Except a listening ear, a smile of knowing sympathy;

Because we share a common bond

As we exchange our feelings,

One the same as the others

How strange that we similarly suffer.

It makes it easy to feel sorry for us.

We agree, that no one knows

How sad and lonely we are inside

And others think that all is well,

Because we have our pride

25.


<u>Fort McMurray</u>


I came to this northern place

I know no one.


People talk to me

Like old friends.


I am still a stranger

But not a lonely one

Some have touched my life forever

By reaching out


Only the ones who live in the north,

Can know the loneliness

Of being alone in the north


And so they reach out

In small ways,

To touch one another

And though you may be

A stranger to this land

You cannot be lonely.

26.


<u>Ashes for a New Beginning</u>

Life's Winter


The leaves have blown away, and the trees are skeletons.

Winter is near, and days are dreary.

No different though from days gone passed.

These sunless days wash over you, in waves of sorrow.

Like an ancient crone, shoulders drooped, an aged tree,

With rivulets of tears raining down to earth,

Following the waterways of age


When all the tears have flowed

And have shown no worth

Then I will give my final gift,

And become one with Mother Earth.

New flowers will bud young saplings grow tall and straight

And children will sit, spent from play,

On my grassy bosom

## A Letter to my Mother in Heaven

Dear mom, It's not a bright and sun filled day

But like my heart, its dull and grey.

Another day of wishing I could be with you

And laugh and chat like we used to do.


Loneliness for your loving face

And for just some moments in your embrace

The longing in my heart cause the hidden tears to start.


As children we are unaware of depths of (love) caring

As many years together, there is so much sharing

It is only when, we age and death is our surmise

That we realize the ties of love that bound our lives


I alone await that day, when the heartache will finally go away,

The sunlight will dry my soul's tears

The disappointments that still have their lives to waste

May someday know how salty love's tears taste

## SPCA Best Buy

### A Pledge


How much is that doggy in the window?

With the big eyes, floppy ears and wagging, tail.

If I can buy that doggy in the window

I'll keep him fifteen years without fail.

I'll organize my holidays to include him

I'll see that he has all his shots

I won't kick him, starve him or leave him, tied up

He'll get so smart as any kind of pup.

Guard the house from prowlers too

And get our, exorcise just we two.

He doesn't care if I'm in a flap

But jumps up anyway to my lap

How much did you say was that pup's price?

I'll pull in my belt and eat beans and rice

Small price to pay for loyalty and love

I'll take that pup, thank the lord above!

## The Workaholic

Your complex system of routine

Leaves a vacuum there unseen

A place where loneliness can thrive,

No space where love is kept alive.


And yet you know and feel your loss

Unable to control your albatross

Your feeble attempts to cure your pain

Leads to nowhere again and again


For the one who loves you, (after a fashion)

There is distant caring and sad compassion.

For the emptiness of love not known,

Lonely year's, and seeds unsown.


Distant man with injured soul,

Deluded into thinking you are whole

Simply being complicated

In a world that you've created

30.


The Workaholic continued


Reaching out sometimes to grasp

But failing and life rushes past.

When you take time for reflection,

Too late! You chose the wrong direction.


You'll be a knife too old to hone,

An empty, house, decayed, alone

Contemplating joys you'll never see,

Will you then have time to dream of me

31.


## Age


Your body counts your age

In years

But your soul stops counting

When you realize you have one.


## Stress


You feel like

You've been

Let out.

Inch by inch

Until there is

No more left to let.


## Post thoughts


Midnight all is so quiet, I can hear

My brain humming quietly inside my ear

Still I wait to put off going to bed

Where poetic thoughts to jump into my head

32.


<u>A Sheltered Place</u>


To live I seek a sheltered place

Where I don't have to see your face

Or drive wildly to keep pace.

A back road house a sheltered place

I don't want a supermarket

Just a country store

I can cook without a can

And raise my bread on the oven door


Now I'm old and slowing down

No need to gallivant all over town

I'm real tired of the old 'Rat Race'

And so I seek a sheltered place

33.


<u>The Indian</u>


I 'live' today

I don't 'like' this way

The shell you see

Is not me.


I am of the forest

And you will never 'know' me.

I make beaded moccasins

From the spirit of my people


I want to be a part of

What they were

I walk silently through the woods.

All that was before fills me

Sadness Because I was born

Too late

My people gone

34.


The Indian continued


I am neither one nor the other

I am what you want to see

While you look at me

You can never see me.

35.

<u>Life is a Dream</u>


Life is but a dream

Of yesterdays all melded

In the molecule of the brain


All mixed up and ready to pluck

Like a plumb, of memory

Bitter or sweet


Life is a dream

Of what's to be

Aspired to be

To have


A dream of love, of hate

Life is but a dream

Swirling by silently

The end of the dream

Is death

36.


<u>Walking Home in the Evening</u>


I step aside, two boys pass, and I waddle behind them.

Unconsciously, trying to keep up

They're good looking youths, carrying their sports bag with ease.

Heading for the recreation center which is on my way

They become farther ahead and I waddle as fast as I can

Wondering where my smart step went

My right thigh muscle paining and my bunion complaining

They're out of sight now without ever looking back

But I'm nearly home.

## Pow Wow

The dance, begin, a whirl of flying feet.

Capes and colors, winging in mad array

Fringes and fur, and girls in Bell dresses

Jingle in time to drums and the chanting

Till dawn lightens the new day


I long to leap into the fray

Fearful they wouldn't let me stay.

Though my blood thrilled to the chants,

I was afraid to join the dance.


Just a person in the night,

They see me as 'just a white'

In my soul I'm 'red' as they

If they knew they'd let me stay.


Who to tell, to lend an ear?

Who would wish to stop and hear?

An old lady, almost white

Red only by the campfire's light.

38.


### The Summers Dance


The springtime left and

The summer dance grew near

The rocks were laid around

Where the firewood

Piled up on the ground

How I loved this northern land

Those quiet smiles that friendship embraces

Make me at home in these remote places

The birches, like me, glowing white

When the drum dance fire lights up the night

39.


<u>A Pet</u>


To have a mate is to pay for food and bed and favors

But to have a little dog, a cat or a canary

Is to have devotion without a cause to Marry


No favors you must pay for, no questions, lies or hurts

A pet will love you always, not in moody spurts.

A pet will allow you time to think or play,

A pet will never leave you if you give it cause to stay.

40.

## A Lifetime

Have I stood at the death bed of Chapin?

No would it were in my time I may.

But that time has passed

Have I held the hem of one single Queen?

No and never would my station allow that to come to pass.

Any yet, though thrones and geniuses were not mine to see.

I have stood beside the grim reaper

Unable to stay his mission

And I have grieved sorely for that.

I have given small comforts,

That was immense to the receiver

And I shone in the reflection of their gratefulness

I have given my love steadfast

To those in need of it

But love is wearing and often spurned

The heart withers when it is

Too many times burned

What am I but one, lowly soul

41.


Give Our Best, continued


Not the confident of Kings

Not celebrated for my enormous and wondrous talent

I am just as I was born to be

No more, no less. Like many other

And when we die we're soon forgotten.

Standing by my grave, someone will say

Who was she? And wonder for a moment

Then walk away.

## A Hundred Years from Now

To Diana and Desiree'


In the year two thousand and eighty-five

You will be one hundred years old, if still alive

Because of love for you, (I hope)

These words will last many years through

It seems a hundred years will last forever.

As in youth, unworried, you seem so clever.

But years roll by, some faster than others

Soon all gone (like Grandparents and Mothers)

It takes only patience and commonsense

To live in the here and not, past tense!

To die is easy and in a moment done

One slip one careless act and you become no one!

A little fear is good for you each day

It teaches caution, clears the brain, fight's decay.

Some fear for your safety you should strive

And if in a hundred years you're still alive;

When that hundredth candle lights in flame,

You would remember me with love

And say my name.

Love Gram

43.


<u>I'll Be Long Gone</u>


I will then be long gone, and only a faded memory.

And if spirits to hover in our midst

I will be with my own Grandmother and Mother,

And we will wait for you and your mother.

When you see the morning mists

Settled along the valleys, awaiting the sun

Could it be, the never ending line of spirits

Of mothers, allowed for us to see,

Briefly as the dawn shines to bring the day

And the ghostly mists must melt away.

44.


### Little Boys


Carefree, happy, scrappy

And treat little sisters mean.

Little girls in barrettes and

Oh so sweet

Dolls and drawings,

Pony lovers;

Dancing feet

45.

<u>Deceased</u>

No more shall the sun shine on your face.

Time was stolen from you without grace.

Flowers bloom now on your resting place.

Just your name in stone your earthly place.


<u>Love and Death</u>

Love and death,

Bequeath us but to wonder.

Until the day

When they are gone,

And split our lives asunder.


When death comes,

We have no power

To stay the hand of darkness

One last flowery bower

For us to see; to break death's starkness

46.


<u>Love</u>


Love, oh love, so sweet, so exciting,

So excruciating when it holds you

In its grasp!

Ah! Love! It robs the mind of sadness.

Throws caution to the wind!

Oh love, a tender pain.

When age has used me up,

And you are tenderly laid away,

To be taken out in evening dreams,

I fondle memories of your sweetness,

Sadness and pain

47.

## Ireland

Far across the ocean, in the prettiest land you've ever seen,

The hills are rolling emeralds, the people can be mean.

They blow up towns and citizens, so the blood runs in the gutter,

Piling up the dead ones, like several stacks of butter

The hills are rolling emerald, but the streets are ruby red,

Because the dear old folks of Ireland have no brains in their head!

## Down the Sewer

Our food chain is poisoned we've all heard the words,

If we could just figure out how to bring back the birds!

The ozone's gone thin and the garbage is piling,

We're rushing to death while our faces are smiling!

As smart as we are, we're a great stupid lot,

'cause we're going down the sewer like a bucket of slop.

48.


<u>The Color of a Flag</u>


"Color the flag." Our teacher said.

I took out the white, the blue and the red.

Carefully I colored our flag of beauty, for I was Canadian! It was my duty!

I loved that flag with its colors bright.

I could draw it and color it exactly right!


As children do, I had to grow.

Until one day I heard "Trudeau."

The color he liked was brightest Red.

We wondered what color was his "Bed."

He banished our beautiful "Red, White and Blue"

And to England he hoped, we would be untrue.

But I'm only a humble poet, you see,

And may end up coloring a fleur-de-Lis

## A Bag Ladies Dream

I sit here in this shady wood,

To pass the time of day

A lonely lady in despair,

No special place to stay.


There is no warming hearth, you see,

No persons place where my heart would be.

If just my wandering feet could stay

A little while in solid clay


There in the woods, a tall strong tree.

I think, "Enough for a house for me."

With such a place, made warm and tight

T'would fend off any winter night


A place to plant a garden plot,

Geraniums and forget-me-not

Window boxes near the door,

And glossy lino on the floor

50.

A Bag Ladies Dream, continued


A little cash for grub and such

A loner doesn't need too much

Is this too much to ask of life?

Without having to be,

Somebody's wife!

51.


<u>Knights in Shining Armor</u>


Where are the glorious heroes

That yesteryears praised and adored?

Have we passed from a time when deeds, were profound

And villains were soundly abhorred


Surely there are heroes in these days

Their deeds, I suppose, are 'old hat'

The newspaper deeds so heroic,

Is something like 'saving a cat'!

The heroes, of old opportunities reared,

They conquered terrible things, people feared!

They were great in a swordfight, their horse's gallant

Castles were stormed by knights, nonchalant.

Today's heroes are those who are raking in money,

Ripping the peasants with tongues dripping honey

The kings, are all gone the queen is but quaint.

If a real hero popped up, the population would faint.

52.


<u>Yesteryears</u>


Oh give me back my yesteryear

When I could run like a deer

My lungs were great and I could swim,

Across the lake upon a whim

Oh give me back a job with pay!

My pension does not last a day.

You youngsters! Stop and think awhile

As you judge the old with a quirky smile

You'd better save some of your pay

Cause you will end up old like me one day

Neither gripe or sulk or tears

Will give you back your yesteryears!

Stop smoking now.

Tomorrow is too late!

53.


<u>For Mourners</u>


Shed a tear for those who pass away.

That is all you can give them.

Remember them on that day,

With love and charity,

For all their defenses are gone.


Soon they will be forgotten.

Their presence on earth

As though they had never been

Be not judgmental

As they did their best

54.


## Grandmother's Love


Come my little ones; my darlings.

Come into my arms, let my love enfold you.

Time will pass, and you will grow,

But not away from love

It is a constant river where memories flow.

Let me hug you now, while you are small.

When you are grown, some bitterness will touch you.

Then you can remember, I love you

55.

<u>Mother I Love You</u>

Mother...

Sitting in your gently rocking chair

Alone

A hundred miles away I pick up the phone.

Recognition of my voice ... I feel your happiness.

How precious you are to me.

How sad ... We live so far apart.

Every good bye ...

Is an unhappy ending

56.


<u>Mother</u>


Where has your lifetime gone Mother?

How did it pass me by?

I don't remember your face Mother,

When I was a child at your side


You were a Mother worth loving.

Home was a wonderful place.

I don't recall in my mind's eye

A picture back then of your face


One day you'll be gone

From my sunlight

A star will be gone from my heaven.

I'll have stepped into your place,

(Dear.)

Will my children remember my face?

57.

## Feelings

How strange each day, to have your feeling in a butter churn

Sloshing about are anger, love, apprehension, duty, obligation, sadness …

What a motley mix! All impossible to discard

One would be enough, but that would be too easy.

Too simple, too much to hope for

And so, at night in bed we try to rest our old butter churn

And give in to hope, that tomorrow will be better.

58.


<u>Judy-Ann and Her Magic World</u>


Long ago and far away, there was a magic glen

Not quite here and not quite there

Beyond the mist in a Faery Fen

There was a magic goose to see

Beneath a magic berry tree

A tiny rill sparkled in the sun

With leaves floating by one by one

There were the smallest houses and a Faery king,

Whispered magic secrets and a magic ring

A little girl, with an enchanting face

Who played in the glen

Of a faery place

Now she's grown

No longer a girl

Still in her heart the Faery mist swirl

Seeking new places for her Faery King

Then he'll give her the magic ring

## Modern girls

The girls wear shorts as tight as skin,

That doesn't hide the shape they're in

Belly buttons sweet and pink

Seem to give the guys a wink

T-shirts cover what they MUST

About an inch below their bust

Those jiggling 'titties' unrestrained

Can hardly keep the boys contained

Some have control more than others

But under the belt they are all brothers.

Like stallions when the mare's tail is bent

They lose their heads when they've caught the scent.

The girls go to court to say they're molested

All dressed like a nun; The case uncontested.

Women want to be liberated that's true enough

But is liberation just revealing your STUFF?

Not really, I think, but you can't change the Masses

And the girls WILL get raped for flaunting their ASSES!

60.


<u>Travelers Song</u>


Stuck in Arizona where the sun is hot.

All the friendly people don't know you're in a spot.

Cash is running low, and the bank is holding tight.

Guess I'll just be sleeping in the car at night

Well it's lovely and lonely here in desert land

When there isn't a single friend to give a hand.

I better start for home or I'll be eating sand

Stuck in Arizona, home is looking grand.

61.


<u>Boy</u>


"Are you alright? Your face is red."

Off you march ram-rod stiff

Miffed by something someone said.


You smile one minute,

Next instant mad

You strike out

Pouting, frustrated, and bad!


Such a big boy, so immature

Undesirable behavior diminishes your stature.

A baby tantrum, so uncontrolled

But your mother loves you

She has a heart of gold.

62.


<u>Spring at Moose Lake cabin</u>


The wolves are howling this late night

The loon across the lake bugling last reveille

As I fall asleep to the crackling of logs in the fireplace.


The Canadian Geese have arrived!

Waking me with their calls like a city's traffic jam

The sun has risen enough

To send her rays in the window

Yawn and stretch, light the little woodstove.

Remove the lid and set the coffee pot in

Soon the pot is boiling and coffee smells good!

Put on the Bologna and Beans for eatin'

Sure is good in the morning sun

Another day has begun

63.


Tree

Long ago on that rocky knoll

Stood a tree, full of life and leaves

That many weathering years have taken toll

And yet it stands, where there's no reprieve

Only wind stripped bark along its length

A memory of what the land once held

Now, the only one to grip with final strength

64.


<u>The Storm</u>


The breeze is sawing through the trees

The evening sky is blue

And distant clouds are billowing

In greys and navy hue

The storm will hit sometime tonight

And little kids will hug in fright

Up on mama's lap, she'll hold them tight

And say, "it be only storming for tonight

The morning will be sunny and bright."

65.


<u>Mike</u>

Our Cocker Spaniel


I'm the master of the house, that's become my fate!

I took the reins the day she showed the other one the gate.

I let her be the boss when she's holding my chain.

Otherwise it is hard to know which one is the brain.

I curl up beside her if I'm not too smelly;

For an evening of popcorn and watching the 'telly

The kids are in bed, they gave me a hug

'Cept, Christopher there, asleep on the rug!

Now don't get to thinking I'm just one of the boys

Can they bark like Hell if they hear a noise?

67.


<u>Banff</u>


The road is wide

Smoothly it glides

In and out, down

The sweeping valleys,

So broad that one feels

Exalted in the wonder

Of this great land


No restaurants here!

No roadside neon.

Take your lunch!

In some provided glen

Spread your fare.


With quiet sentinels

Towering 'round

68.

## Children

Those loving eyes, innocence, in the midst of mischief

Love rushes in to fill my heart,

I laugh at childish pranks,

I feel the pain of their unhappiness

And try to wipe it away with a kiss..

Their heartbreaks are too much to bear.

## People Come and Go

People come and people go,

As so do flowers and melting snow.

We must take all in our stride..

When someone says, "Your Mother died."

I think, "She had her time and space."

Never more to touch her face

There's immortality in death,

And this is true...

As long as someone remembers you

69.


<u>Caterpillars</u>


We used to let them crawl, along our fingers

Up our arms,

Now I'm older, how I wonder; why I thought

They had such charms?

Little fellows creep along

The branches; through the leaves

Black and yellow, furry too,

And what they do is chew and chew.



<u>A Dream</u>


You came to me in a dream last night,

Your face was as I have always loved,

Rimmed by lush brown hair, curled tight

And topped with a wooly toque,

In red and green

70.


The Woodsman


There once was a man

Who lived in the wood

He trapped foxes and rabbits

For furs and for food

He kept a pet reindeer

For company because

One day every winter

He was Santa Clause

71.



<u>Fairies</u>

Peeking through the clover

With her hair up in a curl

The Little Clover Fairy

Could be a dew drop or a pearl

As they play, in fields of hay

The Fairies tire and fly away.


Drifting along on the afternoon breeze

A dandelion puff…

But what no one else sees..

Is a tiny fairy, guiding its way,

To plant the seed firmly

Between, the grasses and hay


Through the woods, so green and airy,

The violets are in blossom.

You may wish to see a faery.

Wouldn't that be awesome!

72.


Fairies continued


See her standing tippy-toes

On slender stem, that gently bows.

It bends so low, and starts to sway,

So the Little Fairy fly's away


Behind a tree, in shaded park

You'll find them where, It's softly dark.

Be sharp of eye and quick of mind.

Be sure you take a look behind.


I know that you may think it's silly

To see a fairy in a Lily

But see the top of her tiny head

As she sleeps on a leafy Lily bed

73.


Summer Day


The grey clouds are moving on,

Driven by warm winds,

They spit on me in passing.

Now, the evening sun shines through the trees

Turning them to gold,

The world is bright once more,

And this story's told.


<u>Summers Past</u>


Back to my youth and soft summer days.

Lakeshore was misted in dawn's early haze.

Walking to town, for a spruce gum treat,

The silt on the road, soft and warm on my feet

Shorts and sun-blouses, and feet never shod'

Sand, water, and nature, and closeness to god

74.




## Family Feud


Into my heart you thrust your heated iron!

Seared my soul, and robbed me of loves warmth.

Alone; To stand where once life was joyful


Happiness has fled my waking hours.

The golden thread of love, like

Our umbilical cord,

Is severed and life's love drained.


Cutting words do not kill when they are spoken.

Death does not come when a heart is broken.

Yearning and hoping with each passing day.

Within, a broken soul has passed away.

<u>75.</u>

## <u>Good Advice</u>

Beware young maids, beware young men!

There's many a swamp to wade,

In search of a sunny glen!

Listen to me now I pray,

Put some aside for a rainy day.

You can never start too soon,

E'er you not see another moon.

You feel invincible!

Nor are you convincible.

You'll live mistakes, so blithely made,

And much reflect, come evenings shade.

76.


<u>Still Here</u>


Life.. Is still with me!

Age and all its kinks and stiffness

Won't let me forget

That life is a small part of Hell

Eating brings on heartburn

Walking pains the heart

Eating beans may not plug you up

But certainly you'll need to fart!

Sitting through a movie seizes up the knees

Winter's chill tells you're old

By causing you to sneeze!

Finger joints begin to burn

There's a bunion on my toe

The only mystery left to me

Is, when's my time to go?

## Loneliness

I hear the owl hoot, in my heart.

Where the deer softly tread,

The shadows of Aspens dance over my face.

And loneliness is my death.

## Love and Death

Love and death tear at the soul

One should be a pleasure

The other a measure

Of peace

But to those of us entwined

Our hearts not inclined

To accept loves loss at the cross

What is life, but love and loss

Flip a coin accept the toss

But deep inside our hearts restrain

Cannot rid us of life's pain

78.


<u>New Bike</u>


I rode my bike like at sixty five

With confidence and ease

Exciting in the cool fall air

With little gusts my hair to tease

The sand and stones and grasses

Whizzed past my speeding tires

I felt again I was sixteen

My legs were screaming Liar!

My lovely car seemed to say, "Alas"

While I counted the money I saved on gas!

"What was that"! A watcher said,

"A funky grandma

With a Hockey Helmet on her head!"

79.


<u>Our Canada</u>


The horses graze on the Hilly Slopes.

The sky is baby blue

And the breeze is rippling,

Through the wild grasses,

Far away the, Monashee Mountains

Below their snowy, peeks

And below, Swan Lake, bordered by tiny building

Sparkles in the sun

The horses graze peacefully

Unmoved by the panorama

Their brains cannot comprehend

This country, the last of the earth's peaceful places

We must be vigilant to what other warring nations

Will bring to our door.

Peacefulness is a treasure

www.ingramcontent.com/pod-product-compliance
Lightning Source LLC
Chambersburg PA
CBHW051344150726
48000CB00003B/1038